City of Canterbury

Six hundred years after Chaucer's pilgrims set out for Canterbury, people still visit the city in as great a number as ever they did in the Middle Ages. Like the pilgrims, most will go to the great cathedral to wonder or to worship. Signs of ancient occupation exist throughout the city alongside their modern counterparts.

Whether your interests lie in cricket or crowns, pilgrims or pageantry, dining or drama, engines or exhibitions, the maps on page 28 and the back cover will help direct you through the medieval streets.

Hail, Mother of England

VICTORIAN MOTTO

The present city of Canterbury really began in AD 43, when the Romans came to settle, although there are evidences of human habitation from the iron age (300 BC).

Durovernum became an important centre of trade.

The remains of a Roman town house, including a fine Roman pavement, can be seen in the Roman Museum in Butchery Lane, but most of the relics of the Roman city are buried below present-day buildings. The Theatre, one of the largest in Roman Britain, now lies beneath houses and streets centring on the junction of Castle Street and St. Margaret's Street.

It is doubtful whether a detailed plan of *Durovernum Cantiacorum* will ever be completed since Saxons, Normans, later medieval and modern builders have all built over it again and again. Ironically, the damage caused by enemy bombardment during the Second World War enabled scientific digging to take place for the first time in the heart of Canterbury, revealing some important archaeological finds.

PRECEDING PAGE:
The River Stour, now a small stream, played an important part in Canterbury's settlement and early life. The West Gate, opposite the medieval buildings, was built by Archbishop Sudbury on the site of the Roman gate, before the Peasants' Revolt of 1381.

RIGHT: *The city walls were built on the foundations of those constructed by the Romans. The Dane John in the background is of undoubted antiquity but uncertain origin – there is no reliable evidence for the source of its name.*

ABOVE: *Viking knife – a bone-handled tool with intricate carving in Anglo-Scandinavian style, dating to the Viking period; excavated in Canterbury. On display at Canterbury Heritage Museum.*

LEFT: *One of the fine Roman mosaics discovered after the Second World War and now preserved in situ in the Roman Museum.*

ABOVE LEFT: *The Dane John mound achieved its present shape when the monument, which records the provision of the Dane John Gardens, was built on it in the late 18th century by an important resident, Alderman John Simmonds, who owned the Bank and the Kentish Gazette.*

He had the whole mound smoothed over.

LEFT: *Roman spoons – part of a hoard of fine silver discovered in Canterbury in 1962 and declared Treasure Trove. On display in the Roman Museum.*

ABOVE: *A medieval city wall still runs along about one-half of the circumference of the old city, following the line of the 3rd-century Roman wall.*

Saxon Canterbury: Cantwarabyrig

What we know of 'the fortress of the people of Kent' began with the reign of Ethelbert in 561. His French Queen, Bertha, was a Christian and the King had given her the church of St. Martin to worship in. In 597 Augustine came to Kent from Rome with a small company of monks on a missionary expedition to convert the heathen English. Partly through the Queen's influence, six weeks after his arrival Augustine baptized King Ethelbert. The King gave him a church which ultimately became the cathedral. In addition, Augustine founded an abbey of St. Peter and St. Paul, later known as St. Augustine's, the ruins of which can still be seen. Until 758, all the archbishops were buried in the abbey which was more important than the cathedral.

Rivalry and enmity between abbey and cathedral increased with the growth of the power of the cathedral and its priory. A great disaster befell Canterbury in 1011,

TOP RIGHT: *The Canterbury Cross – the famous Saxon brooch dated from c.AD 850; excavated in Canterbury last century and now a symbol of the Church of Canterbury; made of bronze with silver panels. On display at Canterbury Heritage Museum.*

RIGHT: *St. Peter's Church in St. Peter's Street, may be of Saxon origin. It is a good example of a medieval town church and contains an ancient Piscina and Easter Sepulchre, a fine old Font and Royal Arms dated 1704.*

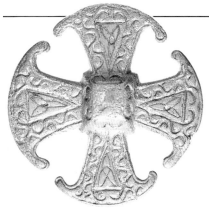

when it was sacked by Danish invaders. The aged Archbishop Alphege was taken prisoner and watched his cathedral being burnt to the ground. He was later murdered.

However, within ten years Canute (a Dane), as King of England, gave and raised money to restore the Christian churches, in particular the new cathedral. In 1023 the body of the martyred St. Alphege was buried there, next to that of St. Dunstan, a man of learning and devotion who had been archbishop in the tenth century.

BELOW: *The Fyndon Gateway, built in the 14th century outside the Saxon Abbey of St. Augustine. Archaeologists have uncovered remains of the earliest buildings and tombs; these are considered the most important monastic ruins north of the Alps.*

LEFT: *Guildhall of the Holy Cross, which until 1978 was a church, is now used for City Council meetings. For many centuries the Guildhall stood at the corner of Guildhall Street and the High Street, until it was demolished in 1952.*

RIGHT: *The Canterbury Pendant – an extremely finely crafted Saxon jewel of gold set with garnets; excavated in 1982 'the finest Anglo-Saxon piece found since Sutton Hoo'. On display at Canterbury Heritage Museum.*

Thomas Becket: troublesome priest

Canterbury's royal castle was built for William the Conqueror, who recognized the city as a strategic stronghold. The remains of the Norman keep are quite substantial. The Roman city walls and gates, in poor repair at the beginning of the Norman period, underwent construction for many years. Today the only surviving medieval gate in the city is the West Gate.

In 1066, the King, the Archbishop and the Abbot were the authorities in Canterbury; the clergy, who were the only people who could read or write, filled all the posts in church or state which required these skills. They were also the largest property holders and were, therefore, closely involved in trade and commerce. In 1070, William the Conqueror appointed a Norman archbishop, Lanfranc. He was a Norman landowner whose liberal disposition protected the city from the degradation brought to Saxon thanes by Normans in so much of the rest of England. For the next 200 years the Archbishop of Canterbury was to become an ecclesiastic and statesman of first importance.

The landed properties of the Church and its wealth were often the envy of royal eyes, and gave rise to generations of disputes. The quarrels came to a head in the reign of Henry II, a proud, wilful man who realised that, in order to avoid offending the Papacy, he needed an ally in the powerful office of Archbishop of Canterbury. When the archbishopric fell vacant in 1162 he appointed his loyal adviser and chancellor, Thomas Becket, to fill the post. Henry reckoned without the stubborn and unyielding character of Becket, whose sole purpose as archbishop was to serve the Church. Within two years arguments between the two men had become so heated that Becket took himself off to a monastery in France. From there he criticized the King, excommunicated important Englishmen and often invoked the Pope's aid in support of his demands.

Just before his return to England in December, 1170, Becket had enraged the King (who was also in France) for the last time, 'Not one will rid me of this low-born priest', he had stormed in the presence of four knights who took him at his word.

LEFT: *Remains of the undercroft vaulting of the dormitory built by the Norman archbishop Lanfranc.*

BELOW: *The Norman Staircase, now part of the King's School, is among the finest in England. The original hall was used as a dormitory for less prosperous pilgrims.*

LEFT: *The Christ Church Gate to the precincts of the cathedral was completed in 1517. The doors were installed after the Restoration in 1660. The face of the building was restored in 1932 and the turrets, removed in the 19th century so that the owner of the Canterbury bank could see the cathedral clock, were reinstated.*

'As the archbishop drew nigh the walls of his city, the trumpets announced his long expected approach and the populace from within streamed out to bid him welcome ... The bells of the many churches poured forth a merry peal as the procession passed; and hymns of thanksgiving were heard ... as Becket entered his cathedral.' This was Dean Hook's description of Thomas Becket's return from exile to Canterbury on 2nd December, 1170.

LIVES OF THE ARCHBISHOPS

In less than four weeks 'the same cathedral and city were witnesses of as black a deed of murder as ever took place within consecrated walls; a deed so black that the shame of it still casts a shadow over the site, and men hush their voices and gaze with solemn look as they pass through the chapel of the martyrdom' (J. C. Cox, *Canterbury*).

LEFT: *This panel is a copy of a medieval painting of the martyrdom of St. Thomas Becket. The original can still be seen, much defaced, at the head of the tomb of King Henry IV in the Trinity Chapel.*

ABOVE: *The Corona, a circular chamber at the eastern end of the cathedral, named after the relic of St. Thomas Becket's head which was preserved there.*

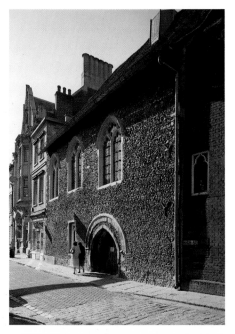

In medieval life 'trade followed the Church', and this was certainly true of Canterbury. The abbey and the cathedral, great landowners, were sources of work for local artisans and tradesmen. Then, with the veneration of St. Thomas, Canterbury became second only to Jerusalem and Rome in importance to pilgrims, who brought wealth and trade with them.

They entered the city through the West Gate and, as there was a curfew at night and the gate locked, many inns and lodgings were needed in St. Dunstan's Street. Many of the visitors slept rough and tents were a mark of the wealthy. Important pilgrims were entertained at the abbey or at Meister Omer's in the priory precincts. In the middle ages, secular and religious holidays were combined, and a pilgrimage was a safe way of enjoying a period away from home in company with enough variety to suit every taste.

LEFT: *The Hospital of St. Thomas the Martyr, Eastbridge (in St. Peter's Street), was founded by Edward Fitzodbold for pilgrims, shortly after the martyrdom. Its frontage is part medieval flint and part 17th-century brick.*

LEFT: *The 14th-century Chapel of Eastbridge Hospital. Services are held regularly for the almshouse community here by the Master.*

In Southwerk, at the Tabard as I lay
Redy to wenden on my pilgrimage
To Caunterbury, with ful devout corage,
At night was come into that hostelrye
... sondry folk ... and pilgrimes were they alle,
That toward Caunterbury wolden ryde.

         CHAUCER Canterbury Tales

The city made itself prosperous by selling trinkets, emblems and other trifles, much as holiday resorts do today, and the religious authorities sold holy items. Almost all the kings of England, as well as foreign rulers, visited Canterbury, but only one, Henry IV, was buried there. In 1376 the popular favourite of England, the Black Prince, was buried near the Shrine of St. Thomas.

Many of the pilgrims would have been vagrants, or sick. They too had to be housed and cared for. Canterbury boasted several hospitals founded for them: St. John the Baptist; the Hospital of St. Thomas the Martyr, Eastbridge; St. Nicholas at Harbledown; the Poor Priests' and others which have long since gone.

In the fourteenth century the popularity of pilgrimages, relics and indulgences began to decline. The seventh and last jubilee of the Translation of St. Thomas took place in 1520. It was attended by Henry VIII in company with the newly elected Emperor Charles V, whom he had met at Dover. The King and Emperor entered the city on Whitsunday by St. George's Gate, the two monarchs riding under one canopy, immediately preceded by Cardinal Wolsey and accompanied by the chief nobility of England and Spain. The streets were lined with priests and clerks, from all the parishes within twenty miles of the city, with censers, crosses, surplices and copes of the richest sort. At the great west doors of the church they were met by the archbishop. Eighteen years later, on 16th November, 1538, this once devout king, Henry VIII, declared St. Thomas a traitor, had his shrine pillaged and all images and references to him destroyed. He himself had already broken with Rome to make himself head of the English Church and Defender of the Faith.

ABOVE: *A medieval badge with the head of St. Thomas of Canterbury – one of the souvenirs of the visit to Canterbury in the heyday of pilgrimage. On display at Canterbury Heritage Museum.*

RIGHT: *Blackfriars Refectory, in Blackfriars Street, opposite the Meeting House in St. Peter's Lane, was part of a Dominican friary. The Blackfriars came to Canterbury in 1220. The Refectory, well restored, is now used by the King's School.*

LEFT: The Canterbury Pilgrims – *oil painting by Thomas Stothard, RA, in 1817. In The Royal Museum collections.*

LONDON

SOUTHWARK   GREENWICH

DEPTFORD   SHOOTER'S HILL

WATLING STREET   DARTFORD

RIVER THAMES   THAMES ESTUARY

GRAVESEND

STROOD   ROCHESTER

WATLING STREET   FAVERSHAM

CANTERBURY

ABOVE: *Pilgrims came to Canterbury from all over the world. The route immortalized by Geoffrey Chaucer was from London.*

LEFT: *Greyfriars House is the oldest Franciscan building in Britain. It was constructed as part of the buildings put up after the arrival of the Franciscan Friars in 1224. The other buildings of the Friary have disappeared.*

RIGHT: *Medieval buildings and the River Stour.*

FAR RIGHT: *Cogan House, in St. Peter's Street, used to be the home of the Mayors and Bailiffs of Canterbury. Dating back to the 13th century, it contains one of the earliest known aisled timber halls and magnificent Tudor carved panelling.*

ABOVE: *Conquest House in Palace Street. The knights who murdered Becket are reputed to have stayed there the previous night.*

RIGHT: *Map of Canterbury c.1580.*

LEFT: *The Butter Market, an ancient centre of city trade, once had a large dome under which women would sell flowers, butter and other wares just outside the Christchurch Gate.*

ABOVE: *Christ Church gate to the cathedral in the early 19th century – print by F. McKenzie in the Museum collections.*

OVERLEAF: *The cathedral from the south-west.*

LEFT: *Carved wooden grotesques above a shop in St. Peter's Street.*

BELOW: *The mysteriously named 'Queen Elizabeth's Guest Chamber' in the High Street boasts magnificent brightly coloured pargeting (1663). It is depicted in a Sidney Cooper watercolour (see page 19).*

'It's a very noble city, the gates are high tho' but narrow, the streetes are most of them large and long and the buildings handsome, very neat but not very lofty, most are of brickwork; it's a flourishing town, good trading in the Weaving of Silks.'

CELIA FIENNES, 1697

ABOVE: *Weaver at loom. From the time of the Huguenot refugees of the 16th century, weaving was an important industry in Canterbury. On display in Canterbury Heritage Museum.*
FAR RIGHT: *The Weavers' Houses were lived in by Flemish and Huguenot weavers who came in the 16th century as religious refugees.*
RIGHT: *Saunders' shop, where Charles II breakfasted in 1664, was a baker's for 200 years. A vast collection of postcards of old Canterbury can be seen here now.*

Canterbury, not itself a port, was on a direct route from the continental port of Dover. Under Elizabeth I wool-weaving was the chief industry of the surrounding district and Canterbury had become a centre for the marketing and despatch of woollen merchandise. The city welcomed a considerable influx of religious refugees from the continent, mostly Walloons and Huguenots. After the massacre of St. Bartholomew in Paris in 1572, the flood of French Huguenots increased and they were given the use of the cathedral crypt for their services. A small French Protestant group still uses the Black Prince's Chantry in the crypt and holds regular services in its own language.

Many of the buildings in the city (particularly shop fronts in St. Peter's Street and the High Street) were built by Huguenot

weavers. Their style is distinctive, with a high gable at the front in which there is a loft door from which wool and merchandise would be raised and lowered. Canterbury names, too, tell of the continental refugees – Lefevre, Lepine, Delahaye, de Lassaux.

The eighteenth century saw Canterbury in modest prosperity. By 1724, when Daniel Defoe visited the city on his Tour of Great Britain, he records that someone had discovered the ground to be very fruitful for hops, and this 'speaking in the language of a neighbourhood, set all the World a-digging of their Grounds and Planting; so that now they may say without boasting there is at Canterbury the greatest Plantation of Hops in the whole Island, something near six thousand acres within a very few miles'.

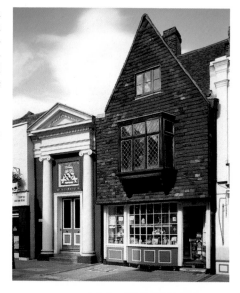

LEFT: *In the 18th century timber-framed buildings were 'modernized' by being faced in fashionable 'mathematical tiles'.*

LEFT: *"Here stood the King's Mill, granted by King Stephen to St. Augustine's Abbey, 1144; recovered by the crown and granted to Rohesia, sister of St. Thomas Becket, 1174."* (*Plaque on the wall of the Georgian building.*)

RIGHT: High Street, Canterbury – *watercolour by Thomas Sidney Cooper, RA, in 1826. In the Museum collections.*

BELOW: *South-west prospect of Canterbury in 1735, by Samuel and Nathaniel Buck, showing the walled city still largely contained within its medieval space, dominated as always by the cathedral.*

'In 1787, an act of parliament was passed, for paving, lighting, watching, and otherwise improving this ancient city; under which, in the space of two years, the whole was new paved ... The streets now, instead of being dark and dirty, and encumbered with signs' bulks, posts, spouts, and other encroachments and annoyances, are open and airy, clean swept, and nightly guarded by able watchmen. And in addition to the above act, by which the city was lighted by number of oil lamps, one has since been obtained by which it is now lighted with gas.'

WILLIAM GOSTLING

To Canterbury by rail

The Canterbury to Whitstable Railway opened in 1830. A relic of this can still be seen in the famous engine Invicta, recently restored and now in the Canterbury Heritage Museum housed in the former Poor Priests' Hospital in Stour Street. It is said to have been the first engine ever designed to draw passenger traffic. The railway had its hour of prosperity and decline, and now no longer exists.

Canterbury is the city which figures in Dickens's *David Copperfield*, though more as a type than in detailed descriptions of actual houses. The nineteenth century saw the return of St. Augustine's College, which had become a brewery and pleasure gardens, to the service of the church, for in 1848 a new missionary college was opened in the rebuilt abbey which had been bought and given back to the church by J. B. Hope. The century also saw the construction of houses which were gradually demolished in the 1960s; narrow streets of poor houses were built without benefit of planning, dictated mainly by the need to provide cheap roofs over the heads of working people. Now the council gives grants to restore the old buildings.

The population of the city has grown slowly, and a faster rate has only come in modern times. It is now about 40,000.

RIGHT: *The opening in 1846 of the railway line via Ashford from Canterbury to London.*

BELOW: *The medieval West Gate with the early 19th-century new gaol built alongside – print by N. Whittock in the Museum collections.*

RIGHT (top): *The Beaney Institute, 1897, named after its founder, houses the Royal Museum and Art Gallery, and The Buffs Museum. This ancient East Kent regiment was amalgamated with others into The Queen's Regiment in 1966, and has been honoured with the Freedom of the City.*

RIGHT (centre): *Passenger's ticket for the Opening Day on 3rd May 1830 of the Canterbury & Whitstable Railway.*

RIGHT (bottom): *Canterbury Station (West), built in 1846.*

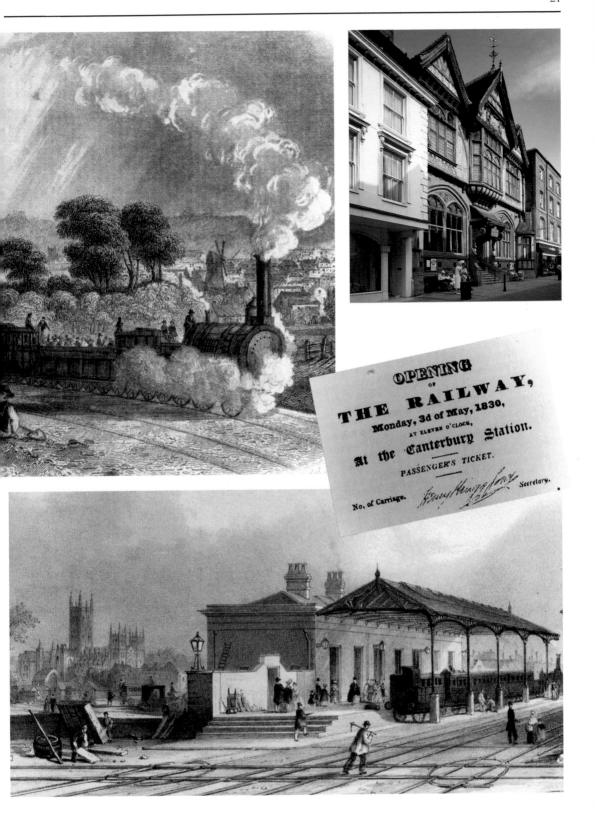

OPENING
OF
THE RAILWAY,
Monday, 3d of May, 1830,
AT ELEVEN O'CLOCK,
At the Canterbury Station.

PASSENGER'S TICKET.

No. of Carriage.   Secretary.

RIGHT: '*Towing the Invicta*', the world's first passenger steam engine, built by the Stephensons in their Newcastle Works for the Canterbury & Whitstable Railway, and here shown in 1906 on its way to be placed on display in Canterbury.

BELOW: *An ancient market until recent times, Canterbury Market is now part of the ring road. Betsy Trotwood was there 'insinuating her grey pony among the carts, baskets, vegetables and hickster's goods'* in David Copperfield.

LEFT and ABOVE: *Joseph Conrad, the Pole who became one of England's greatest writers; he lived near Canterbury and is buried in the city's cemetery. A collection of his books, personal belongings and his favourite writing table are on display at Canterbury Heritage Museum.*
BELOW: *The House of Agnes in St. Dunstan's Street belonged to Agnes Wickfield in Dickens' David Copperfield.*

Canterbury today

OPPOSITE:
Canterbury from the air.

ABOVE LEFT: *The Tourist Information Centre is housed in a 17th-century timber-framed building which has an 18th-century mathematical tiled front. Its leaded windows can be clearly seen from the back.*

ABOVE RIGHT: *The Marlowe Theatre, named after Christopher Marlowe, the 16th-century playwright who was born in Canterbury.*

LEFT: *Mercery Lane. The shop on the left was once part of a famous hostelry called the Chequer of the Hope which in its time housed thousands of pilgrims who came to Becket's Shrine. Most of the Chequer was destroyed by fire in the 19th century.*

LEFT: *The Canterbury Centre in the converted 12th-century church of St. Alphege, near the cathedral, holds exhibitions, slide and video shows about Canterbury's past, present and future.*

RIGHT: *Canterbury Heritage Museum in the Poor Priests' Hospital – a time-walk through Canterbury's history starting with the first Roman town, in a beautifully restored medieval interior.*

ABOVE: *An early copy (1925) of one of the famous Rupert the Bear stories, on display in the Canterbury Heritage Museum. The author, Mary Tourtel, lived in Canterbury.*

LEFT: *The medieval West Gate was used as a prison. It now has collections of arms and armour in the guard-chamber and a superb view of Canterbury and the cathedral from the battlements.*

RIGHT (above), RIGHT and FAR RIGHT: *A medieval church in St. Margaret's Street, now The Canterbury Tales. Here there are guided tours recreating a pilgrimage to the Shrine of Thomas Becket, Canterbury Cathedral, from London; also, audio-visual displays of a selection of stories from Chaucer's Canterbury Tales.*

LEFT: *The Stephensons' Invicta; first passenger steam engine in the world, now in the Canterbury Heritage Museum.*

BELOW: *Armour display at Canterbury Heritage Museum of the funerary helm, sword, spur and gauntlets from the tomb of Sir Roger Manwood in St. Stephen's Church, Canterbury. He was Lord Chief Baron of the Exchequer to Queen Elizabeth I.*

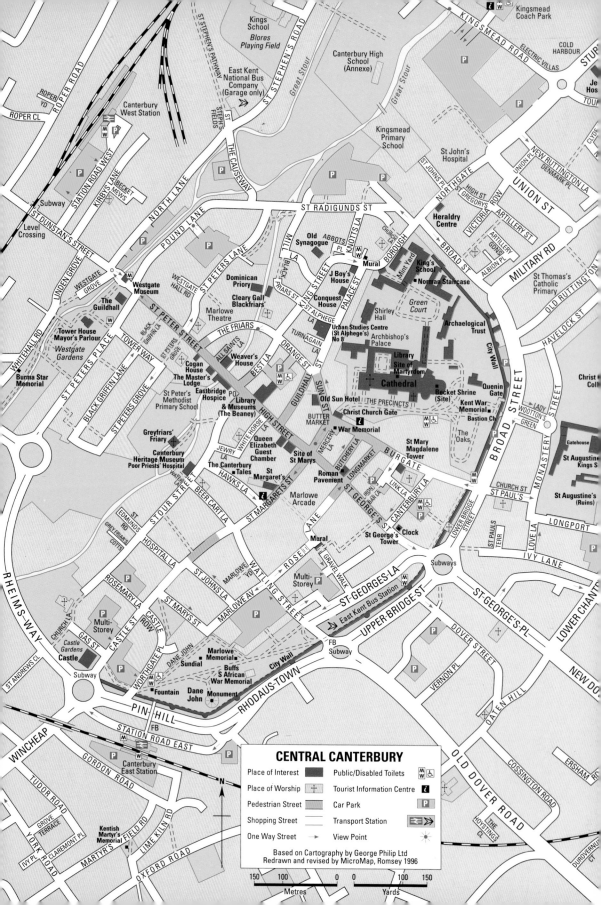